TRUE HISTORY OF THE ROMANI PEOPLE

The Gypsy Stigma: Fact Versus Fiction

Newbury Publishing

NEWBURY
PUBLISHING

Thank you for purchasing this Newbury Publishing book.

Get access to FREE ebooks when you sign up for
our mailing list. At Newbury Publishing we will
only send you emails about free ebooks.

Visit us on our website to sign up at NewburyPub.com.

Copyright © 2022 Newbury Publishing, LLC.

All rights reserved. Except as permitted under the U.S. Copyright Act of 1976, no part of this publication may be reproduced, distributed, or transmitted in any form or by any means, or stored in a database or retrieval system, without the prior written permission of the publisher.

If you would like to use material from the book (other than for review purposes), prior written permission must be obtained by contacting the publisher at permission@newburypub.com. Thank you for your support of the author's rights.

Newbury Publishing, LLC

867 Boylston Street, 5th Floor, PMB 203, Boston, MA 02116

Visit our website at www.newburypub.com

The publisher is not responsible for websites (or their content) that are not owned by the publisher.

Cover and book design by Newbury Publishing, LLC.

The Newbury Publishing name and logo are trademarks of Newbury Publishing, LLC. All rights reserved.

First eBook Edition April 2022

CONTENTS

THE ROMANI PEOPLE: MISUNDERSTOOD MIGRANTS

Who are the Romani people? The Romani people have been historically known as "Gypsies," or bands of travelers that journey across the land without a permanent home. The word "Gypsy" comes from the English word "Gyptian," short for "Egyptian." This comes from the widely held belief during the Middle Ages that the Romani people originated in Egypt. However, the Romani are unique among people groups as they do not identify their cultural heritage with a particular territory or homeland. They do not claim any rights to any of the lands on which they reside or any national sovereignty. Rather, Romani identity is tied to the ideal of radical freedom expressed by not having a particular homeland.

Many countries have their own various words to name the Romani people other than "Gypsies," though this is the most widely known English word for the group. In most countries of Eastern Europe, locals refer to them using the universal word *tzigane*, which is derived from the Greek word for "untouchable" and is considered a highly offensive slur. Most of the names given to the Romani people have negative connotations. The Romani people most frequently refer to themselves as "Roma," which means "people." They are also known as "Rom," "Romany," or "Romani."

The Romani people are an Indo-Aryan group who today live primarily in Europe, with other groups scattered throughout the Middle East, Latin America, and the United States. There are multiple subgroups within the Romani culture, including Roma, Domari, Sinti or Sindhi, Romani, and Kale. There are also a number of other traveling groups that are sometimes lumped in as "Gypsies" but are not Romani, such as the Irish Travellers, the Voyageurs, and the Indigenous Dutch Travellers.

Irish Travellers from July 1954

In the modern world, there are estimated to be 12 to 20 million Romani people, though it is impossible to get a precise count as many do not register their ethnicity due to the history of persecution and discrimination they have endured. Many are located in Eastern European countries such as Romania, Bulgaria, and Hungary. In North America, Canada and the United States are home to more than 1 million Romani people, and around 800,000 Romanis make their home in South America.

Because of their historically nomadic lifestyle and the stereotypes that developed as a result, the Romani people have often been accused of criminal activity such as thievery and kidnapping. They have also been associated with mysticism and curses. There is great stigma surrounding their culture and ethnicity. As a result, the Romani people have been heavily discriminated against for much of their history. They have often been portrayed and perceived as cunning and mysterious. The Romani people have been followed by persistent rumors that they have magical powers, steal from people, snatch babies, and move on to the next town or city before they can be caught. The term "gypped," meaning "tricked" or "deceived," developed as a modification of "Gypsy," referring to the Romani.

Even today, in many countries, the Romani live in slums on the outskirts of cities, often treated as second-class citizens and ostracized by people and governments. In modern Kosovo, the Roma are featured as a star on the flag of the young country but are violently persecuted by the ethnic Albanian population. In Italy, anti-Roma sentiment is very high. After a Romani criminal raped and killed an Italian woman in Rome in 2011, the entire Romani population was declared a national security risk by the government, and Romani homes and nomadic camps came under attack. While progress has been made in understanding Romani culture and people, discrimination is still common. Unraveling the truth of Romani history from the pervasive myths and stigma is quite an undertaking.

In 2016, during the International Roma Conference, the Minister of External Affairs in India stated that the Romani people were part of the nation of India and recommended that the government recognize the Romani community, now spread across over thirty nations, as a legitimate part of the Indian diaspora worldwide. This was just one step in an ongoing and lengthy process of finding acceptance and understanding for the Romani people around the world. In recent years, progress has been made, but the Romani continue to face persecution and discrimination from many around the globe.

Through the centuries, the Romani people have survived by most any means necessary. They became travelers out of necessity, moving from one place to another to escape persecution and find economic opportunities. They have been mystics, fortune-tellers, and palm readers, indeed, but often because they were unable to participate in traditional employment settings. When they have been allowed the opportunity, they have been known as excellent tradespeople, participating in various industries from flower selling and basket weaving to metalworking and goldsmithing, but were often forced out by local craftsmen. While the Romani spent many years as slaves, they have also been muses for artists, inspiring notable works including *Carmen* and *La Vie de Bohème*, and deeply creative, performing as musicians, dancers, and actors through the centuries.

The history and culture of the Romani people are both fascinating and rather tragic, though at times it is unclear how much is legend or stereotype and how much is fact. The true history of the Romani people destroys the existing stigma and shows the people for who they really are—a family-focused group, historically travelers, who have been terribly persecuted but refuse to be defined by false rumors and stigma.

ORIGINS OF THE ROMANI PEOPLE

Because the Romani people have traditionally been nomadic and do not have the same traditional oral and written histories found in other cultures, their history is largely unknown, though there has been much speculation about their origins. For many centuries, people believed the Romani originated in Egypt and were exiled, but more recent evidence indicates an Indian ancestry.

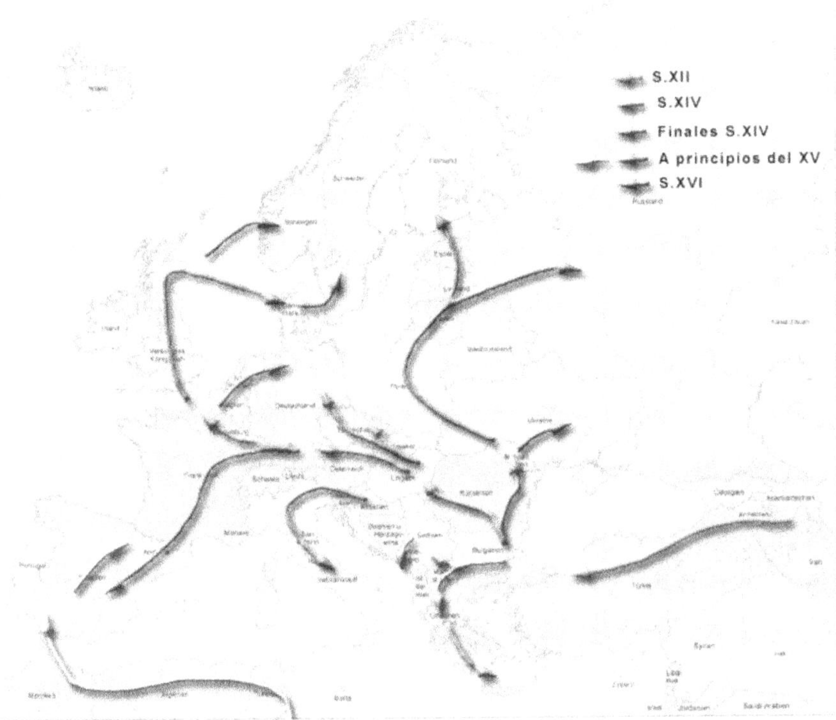

Potential migration routes of the Romani people

While we are mostly unsure how the Romani people left India and ended up traveling around Europe and the world, prevailing speculation has it that the Romani people originated from a low-caste group of traveling singers and performers in India. Others believe that they were part of a small military group in northern India. Still other ideas state that around the year AD 430, a group of 12,000 Romani was given as a gift to King Bahrām V of Persia (from whom is unclear) and that they became well-known as musicians, jugglers, puppeteers, and acrobats who performed in the king's court. Regardless of how the group came together, it has become clear through the years that the Romani people are a distinct ethnic group with origins in northern India.

In 1782, Johann Christian Christoph Rüdiger published his linguistic research that discussed the parallels between the **Romani language** and **Hindustani**, an Indian dialect, pointing to its origins on the Indian subcontinent. Subsequent linguistic analyses have reinforced the notion that the Romani shared a common origin with other groups using the Indo-Aryan languages of northern India. Based on the language they use today and the historical roots of that language, evidence indicates that the Romanis descended from the Rajasthani people in India. Of course, the historical linguistic study is not definitive, and some scholars maintain that the Romani may have learned their language from interactions with North Indian merchants, but most agree that the group has its roots in India.

Genetic evidence for the Indian origins of the Romani people began to be unearthed in the 1990s. DNA analysis found that Romani groups carried large proportions of certain paternally inherited Y chromosomes and maternally inherited mitochondrial DNA that only exist in populations from South Asia, similar to other Indian groups. This, along with the study of a form of congenital myasthenia that is found only in Romani and Indian subjects, points to the Indian ancestry of the Romani people. Further studies indicated that there was a small group of founding Romani people, likely split off from a distinct caste or tribal group in India, which later grew and split into diverse and dispersed people groups.

All of this linguistic and genetic research suggests that the Romani people originated in the northwest regions of the Indian subcontinent, now known as Pakistan, Afghanistan, and Northwest India. They likely have Indian roots based on the genetic and linguistic evidence presented. They share traits with their Indian ancestors such as dark skin, hair, and eyes, along with common linguistic roots.

Most scholars agree that the Romani people left the Indian subcontinent for the Middle East sometime between AD 500 and AD 1100, though some suggest it was closer to AD 1400. It is believed that the people sometimes left of their own volition, but commonly they were taken as slaves to labor in agricultural settings. They were frequently denied the opportunity to return to the subcontinent after leaving and instead were forced to move west, eventually relocating to Turkey, Europe, and North Africa. Another view states that the predecessors of the Romani were part of the Northern Indian military when those soldiers were defeated by Sultan Mahmud Ghaznavi and his troops, forcing the Romani to relocate west into the Byzantine Empire. In either case, it appears that the origins of the Romani people's nomadic migratory status were initiated out of necessity and not choice.

One theory has suggested that the name "Roma" is derived from a form of *ḍōmba-*, a classical Sanskrit word meaning "man of low caste living by singing and music." However, in the Romani language, the word *Rom* means "man" or "husband." It is related to the words *dam-pati*, which means "lord of the house" and may reflect the paternalistic nature of Romani culture, though interestingly, *Romani* is the feminized form of the word *Romano*, which means "of or pertaining to the Roma people." "Roma," "Romani," and "Romany" are all commonly accepted names for the people group.

The first written reference to the Romani people dates from the Byzantine era, during the ninth century. Saint Athanasia of Aegina, a Byzantine saint and adviser to Empress Theodora II, known for giving away all of her possessions, wrote in AD 800 that she gave food to "foreigners called the Atsingani," an early term for the Romani. In AD 803, Theophanes the Confessor wrote that the Atsingani helped Emperor Nikephoros stop a revolt over army pay with their "knowledge of magic." Early text references suggest that the Romani were known as a mystical nomadic group, traveling throughout the empire. They were mostly observed as mysterious, and there are some references to magical powers.

References to the Atsingani disappeared in the eleventh century in written texts, but in AD 1054, it was noted that "Atsinganoi," an itinerant traveling group of fortune-tellers, wizards, and ventriloquists, visited Byzantine Emperor Constantine IX. Constantine had called upon the Atsinganoi to help rid the forests of wild animals that were destroying his livestock, according to "The Life of St. George the Anchorite." Legend has it that Constantine IX hired "a Samaritan people, descendants of Simeon the Magician, named Adsincani, who were renowned sorcerers and villains." They were reported to speak a spell over pieces of meat that they left in various places to kill the irritating animals. This, again, alluded to the use of magical powers that could be used at will to change circumstances.

After leaving the Indian subcontinent, most of the Romani

people stayed within the Byzantine Empire, which included Turkey, Greece, and parts of Northern Africa, for several hundred years. They were known during that period as talented bear trainers, snake charmers, and fortune-tellers. They were also known to sell magic amulets to ward off the "evil eye." Balsamon, a Byzantine scholar and canonist of the Eastern Orthodox Church, warned that the Romani were "ventriloquists and wizards" and were in league with the Devil. Despite this, there were no reports of persecution against the Romani people during this time. They seem to have been viewed more as a curiosity than a danger.

Portrait of Sultan Mustafa II

Other reports from the Byzantine era do not focus on the magical powers reported among the Romani people, but rather on their skills as performers. Nikephoras Gregoras describes Romani acrobats in Constantinople in the early

1300s, saying, "During this time we saw in Constantinople a transient group of people, not less than twenty in number, versed in certain acts of jugglery....they came originally from Egypt....And the arts they performed were stupendous and full of wonder." He goes on to say, "They had nothing to do with magic, but were products of an adroit nature, trained for a long time in the practice of such works." They were described as completing acts on tightrope, trapeze, balance beams, and horses, as well as complex dance routines. There was a high level of admiration for what these athletes could achieve.

When the Muslim expansion under the Seljuk Turks in the eleventh century began, it caused the majority of Romani people to begin moving again, this time headed to Europe. While most Romani left the area, some remained; the men working as miners, ironworkers, coal burners, chimney sweeps, musicians, weapons manufacturers, and watchmen. Some of the women were involved in prostitution, and in 1530, Suleiman the Magnificent issued a decree regulating the sex trade among the group, and in 1696, Sultan Mustafa II decreed that the Romani should be disciplined for their immoral lifestyles as "pimps and prostitutes." Most Romani, however, left for Europe and North Africa in hopes of finding a place where they could live and work in peace.

EARLY YEARS IN EUROPE

It is believed that the Romani people mostly arrived in Europe about seven or eight hundred years ago, in the early 1300s. There is some DNA evidence found in skeletons in Norwich, England, that suggests some individual Romani may have arrived earlier, possibly used as slaves to the Vikings. A more recent genetic study indicates that the Romani people may have arrived in a large wave in Europe in the sixth century. Without written records, it is difficult to pinpoint exactly when the Romani arrived in Europe in large numbers.

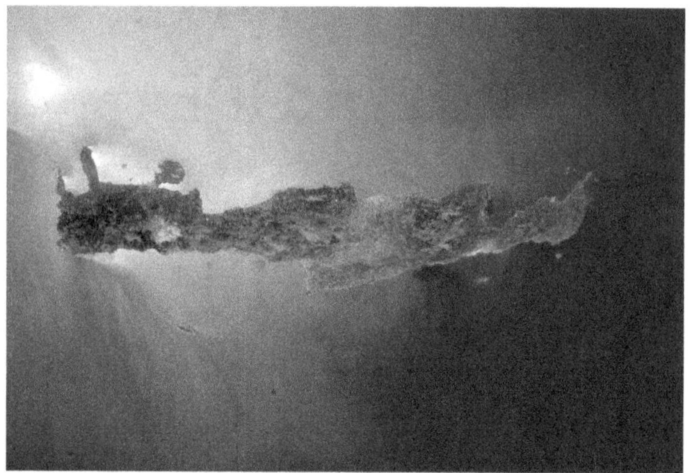

Aerial view of the Island of Crete

The Romani people began to be more frequently mentioned in European texts of the day in the 1300s. In 1322, Simon Simeonis, a Franciscan monk, described a people group similar to the "Atsingani" living on the Island of Crete, by then a part of Greece and the European continent. He described the Romani as "asserting themselves to be of the family of Ham (from the Old Testament). They rarely or never stop in one place beyond thirty days, but always wandering and fugitive, as though accursed by God, from field to field with their oblong tents." In 1350, Ludolphus of Sudheim mentioned a similar people group, whom he called *Mandapolos*, derived from a Greek word meaning "prophet" or "fortune-teller."

Around 1360, a feudal lord established a fiefdom on Corfu, a Greek island in the Ionian Sea. The Romani people there were used as serfs, agricultural laborers bound to the lord under the feudal system. They were subservient and functioned essentially as slaves, completing all the hard labor required to sustain agriculture on the island. Romani were also enslaved in Transylvania, Moldavia, and Wallachia for five centuries until slavery was abolished in the mid-1800s. Slaves were used in the roles of barbers, tailors, masons, bakers, and housekeepers in addition to agricultural labor. Other Romani who were not taken as slaves continued to migrate, entering the Balkans and Bohemia in the fourteenth century. They entered Germany, France, Spain, Italy, and Portugal in the fifteenth century; they continued into Denmark, Scotland, Sweden, and Russia.

In 1378, a law was passed by the governor of Nauplion, the capital city in the Greek Peloponnese, affording privileges to the "Atsingani" people. This was the first legal or government documentation of the Romani in Europe. In 1417, Holy Roman Emperor Sigismund issued them safe-conduct, or immunity from arrest or harm, when passing through the area. Similar documents appeared in Transylvania in 1416, in Hamburg in 1418, and in Paris in 1427.

When Sigismund died in 1437, other documents began to appear, providing safe conduct by the Pope; however, many of these were suspected forgeries. The main papal letter described at the time said that the Romani had been sentenced by the Pope to live as nomads, never to sleep in a bed. The letter also instructed those reading it to provide the travelers with food, beer, and money, and to exempt them from any local tolls or taxes, so they could travel freely.

Most records in the 1400s indicated that the Romani were believed to be in exile from Egypt. In fact, there was a widely known fable during the time that the nomadic people were sent out of Egypt as punishment for harboring the baby Jesus. Despite this, the Romani developed a reputation as thieves and criminals. One report out of Bologna in 1422 stated that a Romani group traveling through had been actively stealing from citizens. It said, "Amongst those who wished to have their fortunes told, few went to consult without having their purse stolen…The women of the band wandered about the town, six or eight together; they entered the houses of the citizens and told idle tales, during which some of them laid hold of whatever could be taken. In the same way, they visited the shops under the pretext of buying something, but one of them would steal."

In 1483, German writer Bernhard von Breydenbach, a German traveler to Jerusalem, described three hundred reed-covered huts outside Modon, "In which dwell certain poor folk like Ethiopians, black and unshapey…the Gippen who are called Gypsies." He stated that they were "nothing but spies and thieves, who claim to come from Egypt when they are in Germany; but it is all a lie… in reality natives of Gyppe, near Modon, and spies and traitors." Often during that time, Romani people were perceived as being spies for the Turks, sometimes because their travels seemed to precede the advancements of the Turks. Around that same time, another German writer referred to the Romani as "Egyptians and heathens."

With increasing suspicion and anti-Romani sentiment, the tide quickly turned on the initially warmer reception of the Romani people in Europe. The Parisian journal in which they were mentioned described them as shabbily dressed and states that the Church forced them to leave the city because they practiced mystical arts such as fortune-telling and reading of palms. In 1497, Arnold von Harff of Modon (Greece) described the Romani as "many poor black naked people called Gypsies" and said they "follow all kinds of trade, such as shoemaking and cobbline and also smithery." Despite their trade skills, Romani were expelled from the **Meissen** region of Germany, Lucerne, Milan, France, Catalonia, Sweden, England, Denmark, and Portugal between 1416 and 1538.

In 1493, the Romani people were banned from Milan, Italy, because they were rumored to be beggars, thieves, and disturbers of the peace. It was said that a Romani child would pick your pockets while his mother told your fortune. People believed that Romani women were experts at witchcraft and casting spells, while the men could pick locks and steal horses like no other thief. Anti-Romani sentiment was strong in Milan, and as the negative impression spread across Europe, the Romani people faced ever-greater challenges.

The 1500s began a time of active persecution against the Romani people. Hermann Conerus wrote of the Romani people in Germany: "They traveled in bands and camped at night in the fields outside the towns...They were great thieves, especially their women, and several of them in various places were seized and put to death." Because of the widespread rumors about the travelers being criminals and involved in mystical arts, they were punished in cruel and excessive ways throughout Europe. In addition, because the Romani traveled throughout Europe like no other people, they knew more than most about the events and activities of citizens in other countries. As a result, they were accused of espionage and suspected of being used as spies. In 1497, the Diet of the Holy Roman Empire issued a decree expelling all Romani from Germany for espionage.

In Spain, the Romani received a positive reception at first, and the Spanish nobility provided some protection. The Romani women were admired for their beauty and charm, and the men were respected as great judges of the quality of horses and were hired by nobility to purchase horses for their stables. However, in 1499, the tide turned, and King Charles expelled all Romani from Spain, with a penalty of enslavement if found in the country. In 1619, King Philip III issued another order sending all "Gitanos" or "Gypsies" out of Spain, this time under penalty of death. Exceptions were granted for those who would maintain a permanent address, speak Spanish, and dress in Spanish clothes. In Seville, Romani were publicly flogged for claiming abilities to reveal secrets by divination, cast spells, and heal the sick by magic.

A Swiss writer described the Romani as "useless rascals who wander about...and of whom the most worthy is a thief, for they live solely for stealing." Starting in 1510, any Romani found in Switzerland was sentenced to the penalty of death simply for being in the country. Similar rules were established in England in 1554, Denmark in 1589, and Sweden in 1637, spreading persecution of the Romani people for just existing far and wide across the European continent.

Romani people were banned from Portugal in 1526, and anyone of Romani descent found in the country was deported to Portuguese African colonies such as Angola and Mozambique. Deportations to the Portuguese colony of Brazil began in 1574, and large groups of Romani were deported there in 1686. At times, only the women were deported, while the Romani men were enslaved and remained in Europe, separating families from one another across the ocean.

In 1530, England issued the **Egyptians Act**, which forbade the Romani people from entering the country and required those living in the country at that time to leave within sixteen days. This was in response to the Romani being "lewd vagabonds, conning the good citizens out of their money, and committing felony robberies." Failure to comply resulted in the confiscation of property, imprisonment, and deportation. The act was later amended with the Egyptians Act of 1554, which ordered the Romani to leave the country within a month, giving them slightly more time to exit, but with the caveat that those who did not comply would be executed. As a result of this act, nine Romani were executed in England in 1596, and thirteen more in the 1650s.

In 1541, after a series of fires in **Prague** that were blamed on Romani people living in the area, **Ferdinand I** ordered them to be expelled. The anti-Romani sentiment continued to grow until a few years later, in 1545, the **Diet of Augsburg** in Germany declared, "Whoever kills a Gypsy, will be guilty of no murder." A massive killing spree resulted, eventually prompting the government to "forbid the drowning of Romani women and children," while offering no protection to Romani men.

In Scotland, the Romani people had arrived in early 1500 and were regarded as performers, tinkers, and peddlers. It is rumored that the "Gypsy King of Scotland," Billy Marshall, lived to be 120 years old, had seventeen wives, and fathered more than 100 children. However, the Vagabonds Act of 1609 passed in Scotland, and in 1611, four members of a Romani family were hanged for not having a permanent address. Eight more men were hanged in Scotland in 1611 for being "Egyptians" or "Gypsies." In 1624, Scotland issued a decree stating that traveling Romani men would be arrested and hanged, Romani women without children would be drowned, and Romani women with children would be whipped and branded.

Coin honoring Stefan Răzvan

The reception of the Romani people in Europe was largely negative, though there were some rulers and some countries that afforded them greater freedom and privilege. In 1596, England changed their stance and passed a statute that allowed the Romani special privileges compared with other nomadic groups, and France passed a similar law in 1683. Catherine the Great (of Russia) granted the Romani the title of "crown slaves," which were superior to serfs but still subservient to the rest of the population. In 1595, Ștefan Răzvan, who was half Romani and had been born into slavery, became the Prince of Moldavia.

Despite some steps toward progress, the Romani people continued to face persecution and hatred in Europe in the second half of the millennium. In all, 133 laws were passed in the Holy Roman Empire between 1551 and 1774 targeting the Romani people. In the late 1600s, at the outbreak of the Franco-Dutch War, France and Holland drafted thousands of non-citizen Romani men to fight in their war. Although they fought for countries that were not their own, those nations swiftly turned on them, and many were butchered during the horrifying ethnic cleansing campaigns known as the "Heathen Hunts" in Holland.

In an act of continued terror for the Romani people, in 1710, Holy Roman Emperor **Joseph I** ordered that "all adult [Romani] males were to be hanged without trial, whereas women and young males were to be flogged and banished forever." During that same time, the kingdom of Bohemia ordered that Romani were to have their right ears cut off, and in Moravia, they were to have their left ears severed. In France, by 1666, Romani men were condemned to the galleys for life, and it was common to brand Romani women before shaving their heads.

In Spain in 1749, all Romani in Spain were arrested in a single night. Their possessions were confiscated, and the men were forced into slavery in mines and shipyards, while the women and children worked in factories. Fourteen years later, they were freed, but in 1783, further legislation was passed requiring all Romani to maintain a permanent address, though they were not allowed to settle in Madrid. The same bill prevented them from working in a number of industries, including trading and innkeeping, which were popular among Romani at that time. Those who continued to live as nomads were to have their children removed and placed in orphanages, and if a second offense occurred, they were to be executed.

In the eighteenth century, some Europeans began attempts at forced assimilation of the Romani people instead of deporting or killing them. In 1758, **Maria Theresa of Austria** began an assimilation program intended to turn Romanies into *ujmagyar*, or new Hungarians. As part of the program, the government built permanent huts to replace the mobile tents that the Romani favored. They also forbade travel and forcefully removed children from their parents to be fostered and raised by Austrian and Hungarian couples. In 1830, in a similar program, Romani children in **Nordhausen** were taken from their families to be raised by Germans.

Russia and Poland introduced settlement laws in 1783 and 1791 respectively, forcing the Romani people to stay in one place rather than continuing their nomadic lifestyle. Bulgaria and Serbia banned nomadic people groups in the 1800s. The Turnpike Act of 1822 and the Highways Act of 1835 in the United Kingdom both prevented nomadic groups from camping on roadsides, replacing specific legislation aimed at the Romani people but still preventing their lifestyle.

In the face of ongoing persecution, some Romani people began to rise in violent protest. In Germany, gangs of Romani men began to form. One gang of twenty-six men, led by the notorious Johannes la Fortun, was executed in 1726, some by hanging and some by beheading. A huge crowd gathered to watch the executions. Another gang of Romani men in Germany, led by Jakob Reinhard, was hanged in 1783 after being charged with murder. Reinhard had led a large group of not just men, but women and children, who were rising against the poor treatment of the Romani people.

As the Romani people faced continued persecution in Europe, their treatment led to an exodus toward a more tolerant Poland and Russian Empire, which promised fair treatment in exchange for taxes. Some Romani also began migrating across the ocean, where they resettled in colonial America and Latin America during the 1700s. Some Romani people were deported to the American colonies, Jamaica, and Barbados under King James I in Britain. Larger-scale immigration to the United States began in the 1860s and continued into the twentieth century.

By 1800, it is estimated that about 800,000 Romani people lived in Europe, mostly in the Balkans, Spain, and Italy. During the 1800s they became well-known as talented musicians, especially in Hungary, Russian, and Spain. Nobility in Hungary developed a tradition of having a Romani or "Gypsy" minstrel play at banquets for their guests, seated next to the host. Musical bands became popular in the Romani culture and always featured a violinist.

In the mid-1800s, Romani music became popular all over Europe. Bands and musical groups traveled to perform, mostly in taverns and markets, as well as at festivals and weddings. Some even went to America to share their musical talents. In 1865, Ferenc Bunko played for the King of Prussia. In Russia, noble families often employed Romani choruses accompanied by seven-string guitars and Romani dancers to perform for their guests.

Unfortunately, for the first half of the nineteenth century, Romani people were still enslaved in Romania. They worked in a variety of roles, such as coachmen, cooks, barbers, and domestic servants, and their masters could kill them for any violation with impunity. The slaves were described as "human beings wearing chains on their arms and legs, others with iron clamps round their foreheads…Cruel floggings and other punishments, such as starvation, being hung over smoking fires, being thrown naked into a frozen river…children torn from the breasts of those who brought them into the world, and sold…like cattle."

The theories of Italian criminologist Cesare Lombroso near the end of the 1800s did not help the case of the Romani people, either. Lombroso subscribed to the idea that criminality is inherited, and pointed to the Romani people, who he described as "vain, shameless, shiftless, noisy, licentious, and violent" generation after generation. And in 1886, there were reports of "complaints about the mischief caused by bands of Gypsies traveling about…and their increasing molestation of the population." In 1899, a Munich clearinghouse was established to collect reports of the activities of the Romani people. The opinion of Romanis in Germany was generally that they were beggars and thieves acting under the cover of entertainers.

While in some areas the talents and culture of the Romani people were being more appreciated, in others, Romani were still perceived as lesser beings. As the world approached the twentieth century, the Romani people were plagued by rumors of criminality and followed by legal persecution throughout Europe.

MODERN ROMANI HISTORY

The late nineteenth century and twentieth century led to some changes in Romani culture and the world's understanding of their people group. By 1893, the census of Hungary reported 275,000 Romani living in the country but also found that most had become less nomadic, tending to gather in enclaves on the outskirts of settled areas. While many continued to perform as musicians and dancers and act as horse traders, they were also employed as brick makers, construction workers, and metalsmiths. Most Romani children did not attend school, and 90 percent of Romani people were unable to read at that time.

In England in 1900, there were about 13,000 Romani people. While most Romani continued to live in tents, they began using some conveniences to make travel easier, such as horse-drawn wagons and trains of donkeys or mules. In England, they worked as tinkers, basket makers, potters, and brush makers. They also provided distribution of goods to remote villages and towns that could not be reached by train. They were valued for their ability to share gossip from other parts where they had traveled. They became known as "Travelers" instead of "Gypsies" in the English language at that time. They continued in their musical traditions, performing at festivals with singing, dancing, and instrumental music. The women also did fortune-telling and palm reading at festivals and carnivals. In both England and France, the Romani would draw large crowds when they entered a new town. Many people longed to see a "Gypsy" in person.

However, not everyone was opening their mind to the Romani people. In 1905, Alfred Dillmann wrote and distributed his *Gypsy Book,* which profiled 3,500 Romani people, to police forces across Europe. He hoped providing information would help eradicate the so-called "Gypsy Plague." In Germany in 1926, laws were passed making it mandatory for Romani travelers to have a permanent address and hold regular employment or be sentenced to two years in a workhouse. The reasoning behind the law was, "These people are by nature opposed to all work and find it especially difficult to tolerate any restriction of their nomadic life; nothing, therefore, hits them harder than loss of liberty, coupled with forced labor."

Some Romani people found a solution by leaving Europe altogether, relocating across the ocean in the hopes of escaping persecution. The United States welcomed a large number of *Ludar*, or "Romanian Gypsies" between 1880 and 1914. Many of these Romani people joined circuses as animal trainers, acrobats, or performers. Passenger manifests from sea travel show that some Romani brought bears and monkeys with them across the Atlantic.

The Romani people began advocating for themselves and their rights on the world stage In 1879, the first known national meeting of the Romani people was held in Kisfalu, Hungary, (now Slovenia) to organize the people and allow them to build a community. Romanis in Bulgaria held a conference in 1919 to organize protests for their right to vote. In 1923, a Romani journal *Istiqbal* (Future), was founded, sharing news among the Romani people.

In the **Soviet Union** in 1925, the "All-Russian Union of Gypsies" was founded, and they started the journal *Romani Zorya* (Romani Dawn) two years later in 1927. The "General Association of the Gypsies of Romania" was established in 1933, consisting of a national conference and the creation of two journals, *Neamul Tiganesc* (Gypsy Nation) and *Timpul* (Time), and in 1935, the first international conference was held in Bucharest.

**Gypsies being arrested and persecuted in Yugoslavia
between 1941 and 1944. 107 civilians were killed
when the church behind them was bombed**

Just as the Romani people were beginning to engage in advocacy efforts and build a worldwide community, they were confronted with the horrors of World War II. The Romani people were a target of the **Nazis**, who murdered between 220,000 and 1.5 million Romanis in an attempted **genocide**. This was referred to as the *Porajmos*. Like the **Jews** and other groups targeted by the Nazis, the Romani people were sent into forced labor and imprisonment in **concentration camps**. They were often killed on sight on the Eastern Front during the war. And in Nazi satellite states such as Croatia, the vicious Ustaša almost obliterated the entire Romani population in concentration camps where levels of cruelty and barbarism shocked even Nazi officials.

In 1940, Dr. Robert Ritter, a Nazi scientist, wrote, "Gypsies [are] a people of entirely primitive ethnological origins, whose mental backwardness makes them incapable of real social adaptation...The Gypsy question can only be solved when...the good-for-nothing Gypsy individuals... [are] in large labor camps and kept working there, and when further breeding of this population... is stopped once and for all." In concentration camps, Romani people were sterilized, worked to death, starved, gassed, and subjected to medical experimentation.

Meanwhile, the assimilation programs introduced in Europe during the eighteenth century continued in earnest in Communist Central and Eastern European countries into the 1980s. The freedoms of the Romani people were severely restricted. In Bulgaria, speaking the Romani language was prohibited, playing Romani music was banned, and Romani newspapers were shut down. In Romania, the Romani people were forced into ghettos, and their personal belongings were confiscated. In Czechoslovakia, Romanis were labeled a "socially degraded stratum." They were resettled in border areas and forbidden from moving or engaging in their nomadic lifestyle. There, the women were sterilized in a state attempt to reduce the Romani population, sometimes by force and sometimes by bribery or withholding social welfare benefits due to noncompliance. Similar sterilization programs were targeting the Romani people in Germany, Norway, Sweden, and Switzerland. In Czechoslovakia, those who did not comply with relocation had their wagons burned and their animals killed.

By the 1960s, traveling Romani caravans were mostly drawn with motor vehicles, and tents had been replaced by small shacks. Many Romani people took residence in slum housing run by the government. Most Romani remained uninvolved in public education and were unable to read. Many of the men worked as scrap dealers, and some used scrap metal to produce ornamental art. Romani women were still known mostly for fortune-telling and begging. Some Romani children in the throes of poverty turned to shoplifting and picking pockets.

Things were a bit better for Romani people who settled in Yugoslavia. There were television and radio stations that broadcast using the Romani language. Some Romani people began to participate in local politics, and a few hundred were educated and became doctors, lawyers, and engineers. However, even there, only 20 percent of Romani adults had attended any formal school at all. Most settled in small towns and worked selling surplus and thrift items.

The first official World Romani Congress was held in 1971 near **London**. The meeting was funded in part by the **World Council of Churches** and the Indian government. It was attended by Romani representatives from **India** and twenty other countries around the world. At the congress, they affirmed a green and blue flag embellished with a red, sixteen-spoked **chakra** as the national emblem of the Romani people, and the anthem "**Gelem, Gelem**" was adopted as the song of their people.

The **International Romani Union** was officially established a few years later in 1977. In 1990, the fourth World Romani Congress declared April 8 International Romani Day, which is a day to celebrate **Romani culture** and raise awareness of the issues the Romani community faces in the modern world. The fifth World Romani Congress, held in 2000, issued an official declaration of the Romani people as a non-territorial nation. The Romani people have made some progress in the late twentieth century in finding acceptance and a voice for their people on the world stage, but they continue to face challenges.

In the 1990s, Germany deported many thousands of migrants to Central and Eastern Europe, where conditions were much worse for them. Romania did the same, deporting about 60,000 Romani people under a 1992 treaty. As a result, many Romani people began to attempt to migrate to Western Europe, the United States, and Canada during the late 1990s and early twenty-first century.

In 1997, a popular Czech television station called TV Nova broadcast a documentary on Romani people who had emigrated to Canada, showing them living comfortable lives with support from the state and safe from discrimination and ethnic violence. The Romani people living in the Czech Republic at the time faced many challenges, including a large flood in Moravia, which left many homeless, and the dissolution of Czechoslovakia, which left many without valid citizenship in either the Czech Republic or Slovakia. After the broadcast, the Embassy of Canada in Prague reported they were receiving hundreds of phone calls from Romanis hoping to emigrate to Canada, and many Czech towns encouraged them to leave, offering to pay for their flights. From the time of the broadcast in August through the end of the year, 1,285 Romanis arrived as refugees in Canada. However, in response to the influx of Romani people, the Canadian government reinstated visa requirements that had been lifted in 1996.

In 2005, twelve European countries launched the Decade of Roma Inclusion, intended to improve the social inclusion and socio-economic success of the Romani people in the area. It focused on setting policies of inclusion in the areas of education, employment, housing, and health, and encouraged governments to address the long-standing issues of discrimination and poverty. However, it met with limited success but was important in that it provided the impetus for the EU Framework for National Roma Integration Strategies, a European Union-led effort to address these same issues.

ROMANI CULTURE
AND HERITAGE

Despite their nomadic nature and their displacement to many countries around the world, the Romani people have a rich culture and strong identification with their heritage.

Historically, the Romani were described as wanderers who lived in tents, except in winter, when they retreated into caves for shelter. They were known to travel without furniture and did not use kitchen utensils. They traveled with just one set of clothes but had lots of jewelry, especially the women. They dined mostly on meat and noodles and reportedly loved tobacco and alcohol. They were known as proud people with loving and large families. They did not engage in any formal education for their children.

Today, Romani families are known to be close-knit, and extended family is highly valued in their culture. Romani society tends to be very patriarchal—the oldest man is considered the head of the household, and all men in the family have more authority than the women. Men and women in the Romani culture marry young compared with many other cultures, and a woman's virginity is prized. Most marriages are arranged by a couple's parents, though the young people do have the right to refuse. Today, more couples are finding each other and dating, but they are expected to be chaperoned and supervised by an adult. The father of the groom pays a bride price to the family of the bride.

Marriages among family members are strictly prohibited, but marriages outside the Romani culture are very uncommon and not welcomed. In the past, there were some instances of child marriage, but in 2003, Ilie Tortică, one of the Romani "kings," stated that marriages must not occur until couples were of age in their country of residence. There have also been instances of bride-napping, in which girls were kidnapped to be married off without paying a bride price, but human trafficking laws have mostly stopped this practice. After a couple is married, the woman joins the husband's family and assumes a caregiving role, and the couple remains with the family until they have their first child, though some remain longer. As women within families grow older, they gain respect for their wisdom and experience but are still considered less influential than men.

Children in the Romani culture remain close to their families. Romani mothers place a strong emphasis on building relation-ships with their children from birth and nearly always breastfeed their children for an extended time, viewing breastfeeding as a gift from God. Births of male children are considered "lucky." Ex-tended family and godparents are deeply involved in raising Ro-mani children.

Families often join with others in bands, or *kumpanias*, formed from ten to hundreds of families, and travel together in large caravans. Within the *kumpanias*, smaller groups called *vitsas* may form among several families, based on common ancestry. Each group is led by a *voivode*, who is elected, serves for life, administers punishments, and resolves conflicts. A senior woman is elected as *phuri dai* and looks after the welfare of the women and children. The Romani people often hold outsiders in distrust, and in some cases they believe outsiders are impure and defile the Romani world.

The Romani people have their own language, Rromanës, of which there are more than 2 million speakers around the world. The language has branched off into multiple dialects given the nomadic nature of their lives. Seven dialects are distinct enough to be considered languages on their own, including Vlax, Balkan, and Sinte Romani. Many Romani people also speak the dominant language of the country in which they reside. Often, the travelers mix the dominant language with a Romani dialect, resulting in Para-Romani speech that is nearly impossible for those outside of their culture to understand.

The Romani people do not follow a particular faith, but often adopt the predominant religion of the area in which they live. They refer to themselves as "many stars scattered in the sight of God" and subscribe to many different faith traditions. However, they do live by a particular set of rules called the *Romano Zakono*, which govern attributes such as cleanliness, honor, justice, respect, and purity.

Many *Romano Zakono* rules revolve around the belief that the universe is separated into what is clean and what is dirty or *marime*. Coming into contact with things that are *marime* is believed to cause a range of conditions including bad luck, sickness, disease, and death. Certain parts of the body, including the genitals, are considered *marime* because they produce impure emissions, and the lower body may be considered impure as well. Clothes for the lower body and all the clothes of menstruating women are washed separately from other laundry. Childbirth is considered impure and must not take place in the home. A mother is considered *marime* for forty days after giving birth. Those who do not follow the rules may be declared "polluted," which is essentially social exclusion from the group.

In the Romani culture, death is also seen as impure and affects the whole family of the dead. It is customary in many groups to destroy all a person's property after death or bury it with the body to prevent them from haunting the living. In most Romani groups, people are buried rather than cremated after death, though this varies within some small subgroups. It is believed that the soul of the person who has died will not enter the afterlife until after the body is buried. And while they may not have a particular religion, the Romani people do have a shared fear of the *mullo*: ghosts and vampires.

The Romani code, or *Romano Zanoko*, is not written down but is kept alive through practice and oral tradition. The main pillar of the Romani code represents the polar opposites of honor, or *baxt*, and shame, or *ladž*. Many Romani believe that it is important to celebrate *baxt* by displaying your success to others and being generous with what you have. For example, making lavish meals to share with guests is considered honorable, while not having food to share may be considered shameful.

The Romani people have typically not participated in formal educational pursuits. A 1989 European report found that only 35 percent of half a million Romani children in the twelve nations studied attended school regularly, and half had never been to school even one time. Romani adults had an illiteracy rate of 50 percent at that time. The Romani people tend to place a strong emphasis on family and community rather than on formal education.

Romani dress and decor are often opulent, displaying wealth and prosperity. Women may wear gold jewelry and headdresses with coins. Homes are decorated with gold and silver along with religious icons, assumed to be tokens of good fortune. Generosity and hospitality are highly valued, and hosts will often offer food and gifts to visitors.

Romani cuisine is varied and often integrates the flavors of local cuisines from the areas in which particular groups live. Historically, Romani food has strong Indian and South Asian influences but also heavily integrates components of Eastern European and Jewish cuisines. Many of their foods are hot and spicy. Some staple ingredients include potatoes, cabbage, bell peppers, garlic, and paprika. Hedgehog stew is a traditional Romani dish in some European groups.

Portrait of János Bihari

Music is a sacred and treasured aspect of Romani culture. A letter from the Queen's court in Vienna describes the Romani as "the most excellent Egyptian musicians." While original Romani folk songs are rare, they do exist. Most are vocal performances accompanied by tongue clicks, handclapping, and playing of spoons or other simple instruments. It is also understood that the style and performances of Romani musicians influenced classical European composers such as Franz Liszt and Johannes Brahms, along with impacting the musical underpinnings of bolero and jazz. The first famous Romani violinist, Janos Bihari, performed at the Congress of Vienna in 1814.

The Romani people are known not only for their music but also for their styles of dance that accompany different types of music. The Spanish flamenco and traditional Egyptian dances are believed to have originated from the Romani people. Romani have been known to perform Roman Havasi, a type of Turkish folk dance set to Byzantine music, reaching back to their historic roots. Some groups are experts at Cocek, a type of dance originating in Ottoman military bands. Belly dancing has also been part of the Romani culture.

Music and dance are well-known aspects of the culture of the Romani people. However, they have historically been and continue to be involved in a number of performing arts, including theater and cinema, visual arts, literature, puppeteering, ventriloquism, and many others, and they have also made their way into politics. There are a number of celebrities with Romani roots, including actors Charlie Chaplin, Yul Brynner, Michael Caine, and Rita Hayworth; painter Pablo Picasso; and the "King of Rock and Roll," Elvis Presley. Successful athletes including wrestlers, boxers, soccer and hockey players have come from Romani ancestry. The thirteenth and twenty-first presidents of Brazil, Washington Luis and Juscelino Kubitschek, are also reportedly of Romani descent.

THE GYPSY STIGMA: FACT VS. FICTION

After being misunderstood for centuries, it is no wonder that the Romani people continue to be haunted by rumors and myths about their culture and lifestyle. Here are just some of the myths about the Romani people, and the truth that may set the stigma to rest.

Myth: The Romani people are criminals

One of the most pervasive myths about the Romani people is that there is a high prevalence of criminality among them. For centuries, the group has been characterized as thieving, tricky, pickpocketing, and kidnapping criminals. However, research published in 2021 states that Romani people are much more likely to be victims of crime than to commit crimes themselves. The hate crimes against their group have persisted for hundreds of years, resulting in hundreds of thousands of deaths. Crime rates among Romani and non-Romani people are equivalent, though the Romani are overrepresented in prisons and less likely to have a successful transition back to civilian life once they are released. While it is true that some individual criminals, and even some organized crime groups, exist within the Romani culture, that is true of all cultures and is no more prevalent among their group.

Myth: The Romani travel so they do not have to have jobs or pay taxes

Romani travelers work and pay taxes just like anyone else. In fact, the Romani people are known for having a very strong work ethic, and often, teenagers begin working much younger than in other cultures, learning the trades passed down through their families. Many Romani do prefer self-employment as it allows for travel and complies with visa rules more easily.

And Romani do pay taxes. Any traveler living on land owned by a municipality or private site will need to pay rent and any applicable taxes. They pay sales tax in the places they visit. And if they are legally employed or self-employed, they pay income taxes. By not purchasing permanent homes, they avoid property taxes, but the same is true of anyone who rents a home.

Myth: Romani are dirty and leave trash everywhere they go

Romani culture places a very high value on cleanliness as they subscribe to the Romano guidelines. Typically, the insides of caravans and Romani houses are very clean and tidy. They have very strict rules about personal hygiene and food preparation. Many travelers use the area immediately outside their homes or caravans as a workspace, so it may appear untidy from the outside at times, but there is great honor in keeping a tidy home.

Due to rules governing authorized camping, at times caravans may need to move quickly and leave a mess behind if they are asked to move on in the middle of the night. In addition, because of continuing discrimination against travelers, at times they are targeted by locals who dump waste in their areas and place blame on the Romani.

Myth: The Romani are genetically programmed to wander

Very few nomadic cultures in history have chosen a life of wandering out of desire, and the need to travel is not a genetically embedded trait. The nomadic life of the Romani people was created by a combination of factors: most prominently, the need to follow economic opportunities and to flee persecution. Romani have adapted to the need to be constantly on the move by working within trades that have highly transferable skills that may be used anywhere, and they have always sought out the safest places for their people to reside, considering the global stigma against their people.

In recent years, as their people group has become more accepted, many Romani have started to remain in one place. Amnesty International reports that 90 percent of "Gypsies" around the world now live in permanent homes. In some areas, such as the United Kingdom, the nomadic lifestyle continues among about 50 percent of Romanis, but many more are buying homes and putting down roots than in previous years.

Myth: The Romani do not want to educate their children

The Romani people have traditionally not engaged in formal education for their children, though that has changed somewhat in recent years. However, Romani children who attend public school face some challenges. In a survey in the United Kingdom, three out of every four Romani children who went to public school said they were bullied because of their cultural background. In some areas of Eastern Europe, Romani children are placed in separate classes and do not receive the same level of education as other students. The Romani people understand the value of literacy and formal education, but reaching those goals is difficult given the challenges they face.

Myth: The Romani are mystical and practice magic

Many common perceptions of traveling Romani are that they engage in magical arts such as tarot reading, crystal balls, palm reading, and fortune-telling. While it is true that part of Romani history involves using these arts to make a living in the circuses and carnivals in which they performed, and while some subgroups still specialize in fortune-telling, a typical Romani person is no more likely to be a mystic than anyone else. The Romani people participate in any number of religions that would forbid or discourage the use of magic or mystical arts, and many do not subscribe to mystical beliefs. They cannot curse anyone, read someone's mind, or channel spirits any more than the next person.

Myth: The Romani people are promiscuous

In fact, the Romani place a high value on modesty. In some groups, discussions involving sexuality are forbidden, and some groups have particular rules governing how much skin can be revealed in public. As many Romani people adopt aspects of the surrounding culture, their dress may vary, but most value modesty. They are very family-focused and marry young, and a woman's virginity is prized. Women are typically not even permitted to discuss menstruation. Promiscuity is not rampant in Romani groups.

THE ROMANI PEOPLE OF THE NEW MILLENNIUM

Today, between 5 and 6 million Romani people are living in Europe, and there are 12 to 20 million Romani worldwide. Most live in Romania (about 1 million), while many are distributed among Bulgaria, Hungary, Russia, Spain, Turkey, Serbia, and Slovakia. There are anywhere from 100,000 to 1 million Romani people in the United States. Other Romani groups are scattered across Europe, North America, and Latin America.

The Romani people of the new millennium are faced with the challenges of preserving their culture and lifestyle while attempting to integrate into the modern world. More Romani young people are receiving public education and are exposed to the Internet, social media, and popular culture, and have frequent interactions with others outside Romani culture.

In some areas, especially in Western Europe, Romani families still work mostly in circuses and fairgrounds, continuing in traditional mystical roles like fortune-telling and palm reading. Some also continue in musical and dance performance roles. However, in many countries, they sell used cars and goods and operate repair services, working across a variety of industries in an attempt to make a living. More Romani people are choosing to settle into permanent homes, no longer forced out of cities or countries by systemic discrimination and persecution. However, they continue to face the stigma they have carried with them for centuries.

While conditions have improved for many Romani people, they still face pervasive stigma and discrimination. A survey by the European Union Agency for Fundamental Rights recently found that half of Romani people said they were discriminated against at least once in the last year, based on their ethnicity. Romani people continue to have more difficulty finding permanent jobs, with nearly half of employers stating they do not believe a Romani person would be offered a job in their company.

The Romani people also have greater difficulty participating in formal education and accessing human services because of their cultural background. A report found that 52 percent of Romani children in Eastern Europe are placed in schools for students who are "mentally handicapped," often without any type of assessment or notification to the parents of this specific school setting.

Worse, there continues to be outright violence against Romani people in many areas. A report in *The Guardian* in 2000 outlined a number of crimes against Romani that occurred within just a few weeks of one another. On March 2, 2000, four policemen in Romania punched and beat a Romani man to the ground as he was surrounded by other Romani onlookers. Twenty-five more police were called in to disperse the crowd and it turned violent, with police beating Romani people, calling out racial slurs, and spraying tear gas at children. One day later, near Rome, a "camp for nomads" filled with Romani people was invaded in the early morning hours. All residents were detained, permits were checked, and fifty-six people were immediately deported to Bosnia. Another operation occurred the following day near Rome. In the Czech Republic that year, the city of Ústí nad Labem built a wall around the "Gypsy ghetto," creating an enclosure around the neighborhood to keep them separate from the rest of the city's dwellers.

A 2003 report from the United Nations provided strong statistical evidence regarding the extent of the challenges faced by the Romani people in modern society. These include illiteracy, high rates of infant mortality, unemployment, and segregation in education. They also frequently face hunger and malnutrition, poor housing without sanitation or adequate plumbing, and limited access to healthcare. All these factors mean the Romani people have the shortest life expectancy in all of Europe.

Despite all the challenges they face, there is hope for the Romani people going into the future. They have strong cultural connections and values, and there is increasing understanding and awareness of their plight. The Decade of Roma Inclusion from 2005 to 2015 committed member nations to improving the welfare of the Romani people in their countries. The European Court of Human Rights ended school segregation practices in Eastern Europe. Public health policies are being developed and implemented to address the group's lack of access to good healthcare. Hundreds of human rights organizations are increasing awareness of the stigma the Romani people have faced and helping encourage legislative change to support the people group.

**The Gypsy Girl, an almost 2,000-year-old mosaic
of a young Romani girl**

Thank you for purchasing this Newbury Publishing ebook.

Don't forget, get access to FREE ebooks when you sign up for our mailing list. At Newbury Publishing we will only send you emails about free ebooks.

CLICK HERE TO SIGN UP

Find more of our books here